Gustav
HOLST

FIRST SUITE IN E-FLAT
Op. 28 No. 1
(Richard W. Sargeant, Jr.)

Study Score
Partitur

SERENISSIMA MUSIC, INC.

Gustav Holst's first work for band was composed in 1909 and originally entitled "Suite in E-flat". The occasion or ensemble for which it was written is unknown. Although there is no record of a performance until the official premiere given in 1920 at the Royal Military School of Music, it is likely that there was at least a reading before that date as Holst made a number of revisions to the work - including a title change to "First Suite in E-flat for Military Band". Other revisions included thinning out of textures in the second movement, and some re-orchestration elsewhere. The work's publication (Boosey & Co.) did not take place until 1921, a dozen years after its creation, and then only in the form of the condensed score and set of parts typically issued in the era.

In 1909 there was no standardization of concert band instrumentation as there is today. While this situation caused difficulties for other composers Holst employed an elastic scoring method so the work could be performed by the largest number of possible instrumental combinations available in bands of the era. Ingenious as this is, several of the instruments common in Holst's time are obsolete. These include the D-flat piccolo, D-flat flute, E-flat trumpets and B-flat baritone. While C piccolos and flutes have replaced their D-flat counterparts, the E-flat trumpet of Holst's era was the military band counterpart to the orchestral Trumpets in F - thus closer in tube-length and sound to the natural trumpets of Beethoven's time than the smaller instruments (pitched in B-flat and C) now encountered. The B-flat baritone specified in Holst's manuscript was an instrument of the cornet family which was similar in many respects to the tenor saxhorns found in European bands. Because of the improvements in instrument design and functionality, substitutions are needed to render the work playable for modern bands.

In 1948 Boosey & Hawkes issued a new set of parts and a full score for the first time. Since the manuscript was lost at the time, the original 1921 parts were used to create the score, substitutions were made for the obsolete instruments, several additional instruments were added to increase the work's appeal to American bands. The 1948 edition was thus something quite different from Holst's original score, written for a considerably smaller ensemble (20-30 players at most). Holst would have expected doubling only on the parts for flutes (if any), clarinets and cornets, the remainder being one player per part. As originally scored, the work could be performed with only 19 players plus percussion. Important parts were cued in other instruments and even some of the core 19 were cross-cued as well. Holst was sometimes careless with the scoring of ad lib. parts assigned to harmony.

The Instruments added in the 1948 score were E-flat alto clarinet, B-flat contrabass clarinet, E-flat baritone saxophone, B-flat bass saxophone, and flügelhorns. Along with the additions the Boosey & Hawkes editors omitted the string bass and reorganized the original 2 cornets and 4 trumpets into 4 parts (2 cornets, 2 trumpets) - though this did not cause any major issues as there was much doubling among the 6 original parts. The disposition of the original B-flat baritone presents a different set of problems: much of this part was split between the alto clarinet and the baritone saxophone in the 1948 score. This was probably done in response to an official 1921 directive from the Directors of Music of the military bands to replace the B-flat baritone with the B-flat tenor saxophone. Since Holst had already included a tenor saxophone part, the Boosey & Hawkes editors found it necessary to re-assign the B-flat baritone to the instruments mentioned above. Unfortunately, neither of the substitution instruments resembles the B-flat baritone in timbre or power. The String Bass part was most likely omitted because American High School bands were unlikely to have one available, and Holst himself designated it as an "ad lib." instrument.

For the present score, the editor has made every attempt to remain as faithful as possible to Holst's original manuscript, keeping the necessary changes in the spirit Holst intended. The added parts in the 1948 Boosey & Hawkes score have been eliminated with the exception of the baritone saxophone. This added part has been changed drastically from the one found in the 1948 publication, which was used partially as a substitute for some of the B-flat baritone part and elsewhere doubles many of the brass lines. The new baritone saxophone part is more idiomatic and more in keeping with Holst's intentions as well. The other major change is found in the euphonium part. Here the original B-flat baritone part appears as the top half of a divisi part. The cornet and trumpet parts remain the same as in the original Boosey parts with only minor changes to cover anything missing from the original. Changes and corrections to produce consistent articulations and phrasing have been made without comment.

Richard W. Sargeant, Jr.
December, 2011

Holst's Original Instrumentation

Flute / Piccolo in D-flat

2 Clarinets in E-flat (2nd ad lib.)

2 Oboes (ad lib.)

Solo Clarinet in B-flat

1st Clarinets in B-flat *ripieno*

2nd Clarinets in B-flat

3rd Clarinets in B-flat

[Alto] Saxophone in E-flat (ad lib.)

[Tenor] Saxophone in B-flat (ad lib.)

Bass Clarinet in B-flat (ad lib.)

2 Bassoons (2nd ad lib.)

1st Cornets in B-flat

2nd Cornets in B-flat

2 Trumpets in E-flat (ad lib.)

2 Trumpets in B-flat (ad lib.)

2 Horns in E-flat

2 Horns in F (ad lib.)

Baritone in B-flat (ad lib.)

2 Tenor Trombones (2nd ad lib.)

Bass Trombone

Euphonium in B-flat

Bombardons (Tubas)

String Bass (ad lib.)

Timpani (ad lib.)

Percussion

(Bass Drum, Cymbals, Side Drum, Triangle, Tambourine)

Duration: ca. 10 minutes

First documented performace: June 23, 1920
Twickenham, Royal Military School of Music: Kneller Hall
Col. J.A.C. Somerville, conductor

ISBN: 978-160874-051-2
Printed in the USA
First Printing: December, 2011

FIRST SUITE FOR MILITARY BAND
in E♭

1. Chaconne

Gustav Holst
Edited by Richard W. Sargeant, Jr.

16
25
Picc.
Fl.
Ob. 1 2
a2
pp legato
cresc.
mf
Eb Cl. 1 2
Cl. 1 2 3
B. Cl.
Bn. 1 2
Alto Sax.
Ten. Sax.
Bari. Sax.
Cor. 1 2
solo
Tpt. 1 2
Hn. 1 2 3 4
Trb. 1 2
1. solo
Bass
Eph.
Basses
S. B.
pp
Timp.
Per.
Cymb. B. D.

27
Picc.
Fl.
Ob. 1 2
E♭ Cl. 1 2
Cl. 1 2 3
B. Cl.
Bn. 1 2
Alto Sax.
Ten. Sax.
Bari. Sax.
Cor. 1 2
Tpt. 1 2
Hn. 1 2 3 4
Trb. 1 2
Bass
Eph.
Basses
S. B.
Timp.
Per.
Cymb. B. D.
a2
cresc.
mf cresc.
tutti
div.
S. D.
f
mf

41 Brilliante
36
Picc.
Fl.
Ob. 1 2
E♭ Cl. 1 2
Cl. 1 2 3
B. Cl.
Bn. 1 2
Alto Sax.
Ten. Sax.
Bari. Sax.
cresc.
ff
41 Brilliante
36
Cor. 1 2
Tpt. 1 2
Hn. 1 2 3 4
Trb. 1 2
Bass
Eph.
Basses
S. B.
Timp.
Per.
Cymb. B. D.

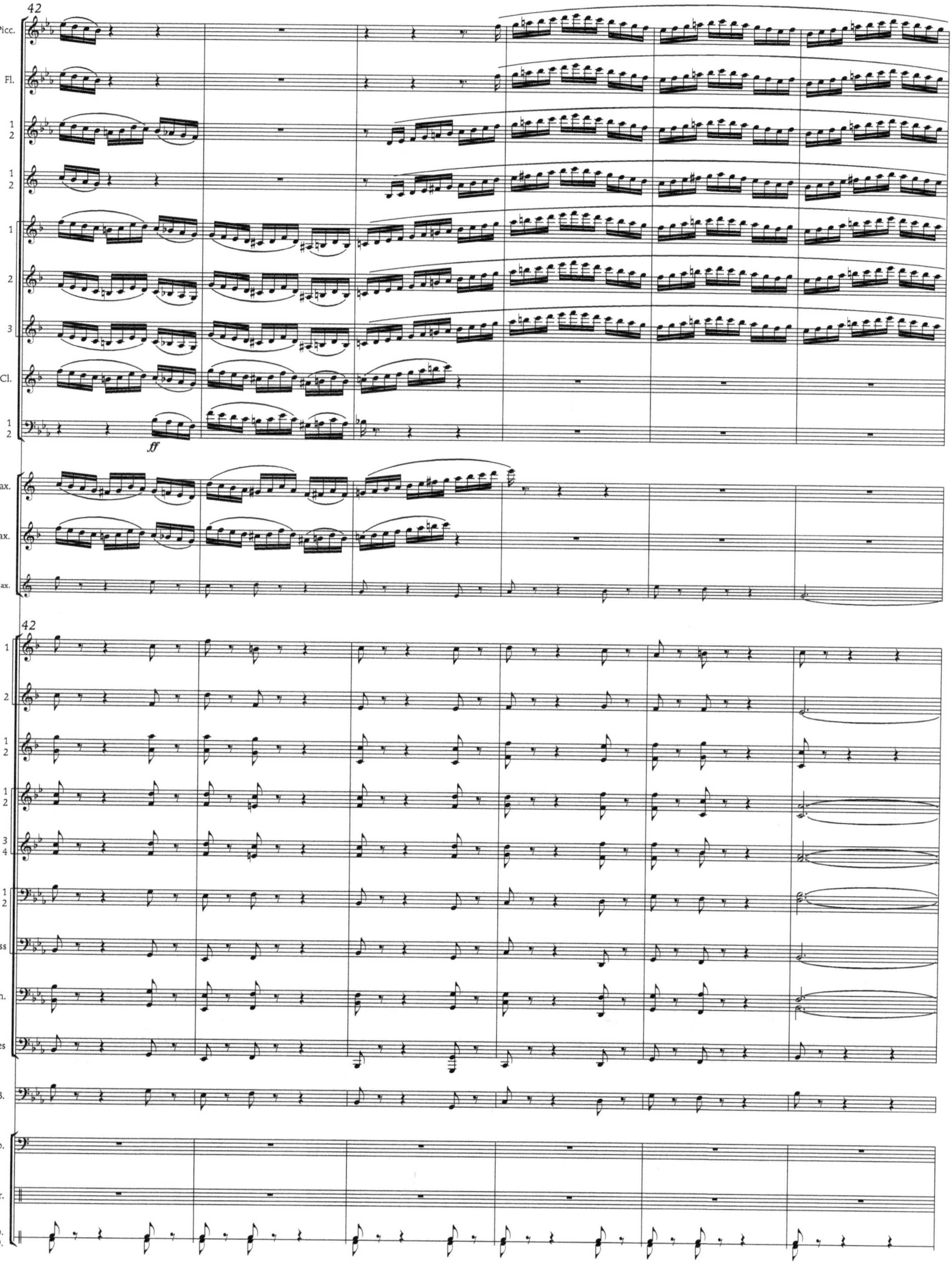
42
Picc.
Fl.
Ob. 1 2
E♭ Cl. 1 2
Cl. 1 2 3
B. Cl.
Bn. 1 2
ff
Alto Sax.
Ten. Sax.
Bari. Sax.
42
Cor. 1 2
Tpt. 1 2
Hn. 1 2 3 4
Trb. 1 2 Bass
Eph.
Basses
S. B.
Timp.
Per.
Cymb. B. D.

48
Pesante
57
Picc.
Fl.
Ob. 1 2
E♭ Cl. 1 2
Cl. 1 2 3
B. Cl.
Bn. 1 2
ff
dim.
p
Alto Sax.
Ten. Sax.
Bari. Sax.
ten.
div.
a2
1. solo
Cor. 1 2
Tpt. 1 2
Hn. 1 2 3 4
Trb. 1 2
Bass
Eph.
Basses
S. B.
Timp.
Per.
Cymb. B. D.

58
Picc.
Fl.
solo
Ob. 1 2
1. solo
E♭ Cl. 1 2
1.
Cl. 1 2 3
B. Cl.
Bn. 1 2
Alto Sax.
solo
Ten. Sax.
Bari. Sax.
58
Cor. 1 2
Tpt. 1 2
Hn. 1 2 3 4
Trb. 1 2
Bass
Eph.
Basses
S. B.
Timp.
Per.
Cymb. B. D.

68
Picc.
Fl.
Ob. 1 2
E♭ Cl. 1 2
Solo Cl.
Cl. 1 2 3
B. Cl.
Bn. 1 2
Alto Sax.
Ten. Sax.
Bari. Sax.
Cor. 1 2
Tpt. 1 2
Hn. 1 2 3 4
Trb. 1 2
Bass
Eph.
Basses
S. B.
Timp.
Per.
Cymb. B. D.
a2
1.

80
81
Picc.
Fl.
Ob. 1 2
E♭ Cl. 1 2
Solo Cl.
Cl. 1 2 3
B. Cl.
Bn. 1 2
a2
p pesante
p
Alto Sax.
Ten. Sax.
Bari. Sax.
Cor. 1 2
Tpt. 1 2
Hn. 1 2 3 4
Trb. 1 2
Bass
Eph.
unis.
div.
Basses
S. B.
Timp.
Per.
Cymb. B. D.
(with timp. sticks)
pp

93
97
Picc.
Fl.
Ob. 1 2
E♭ Cl. 1 2
Cl. 1 2 3
B. Cl.
Bn. 1 2
Alto Sax.
Ten. Sax.
Bari. Sax.
Cor. 1 2
Tpt. 1 2
Hn. 1 2 3 4
Trb. 1 2
Bass
Eph.
Basses
S. B.
Timp.
Per.
Cymb. B. D.
tutti
a2
1.
S. D.
p
pp
ppp
cresc. poco a poco
p cresc. poco a poco

114 Maestoso
106
Picc.
Fl.
Ob. 1 2
E♭ Cl. 1 2
Cl. 1 2 3
B. Cl.
Bn. 1 2
Alto Sax.
Ten. Sax.
Bari. Sax.
106
114 Maestoso
div.
Cor. 1 2
Tpt. 1 2
Hn. 1 2 3 4
Trb. 1 2
a2
Bass
Eph.
Basses
S. B.
Timp.
Per.
Cymb. B. D.
ff

117
rit. al fine
Picc.
Fl.
Ob. 1 2
E♭ Cl. 1 2
Cl. 1 2 3
B. Cl.
Bn. 1 2
Alto Sax.
Ten. Sax.
Bari. Sax.
117
rit. al fine
unis.
div.
Cor. 1 2
a2
Tpt. 1 2
Hn. 1 2 3 4
Trb. 1 2
Bass
unis.
Eph.
Basses
S. B.
ff
Timp.
Per.
fff
Cymb. B. D.
ff

2. Intermezzo

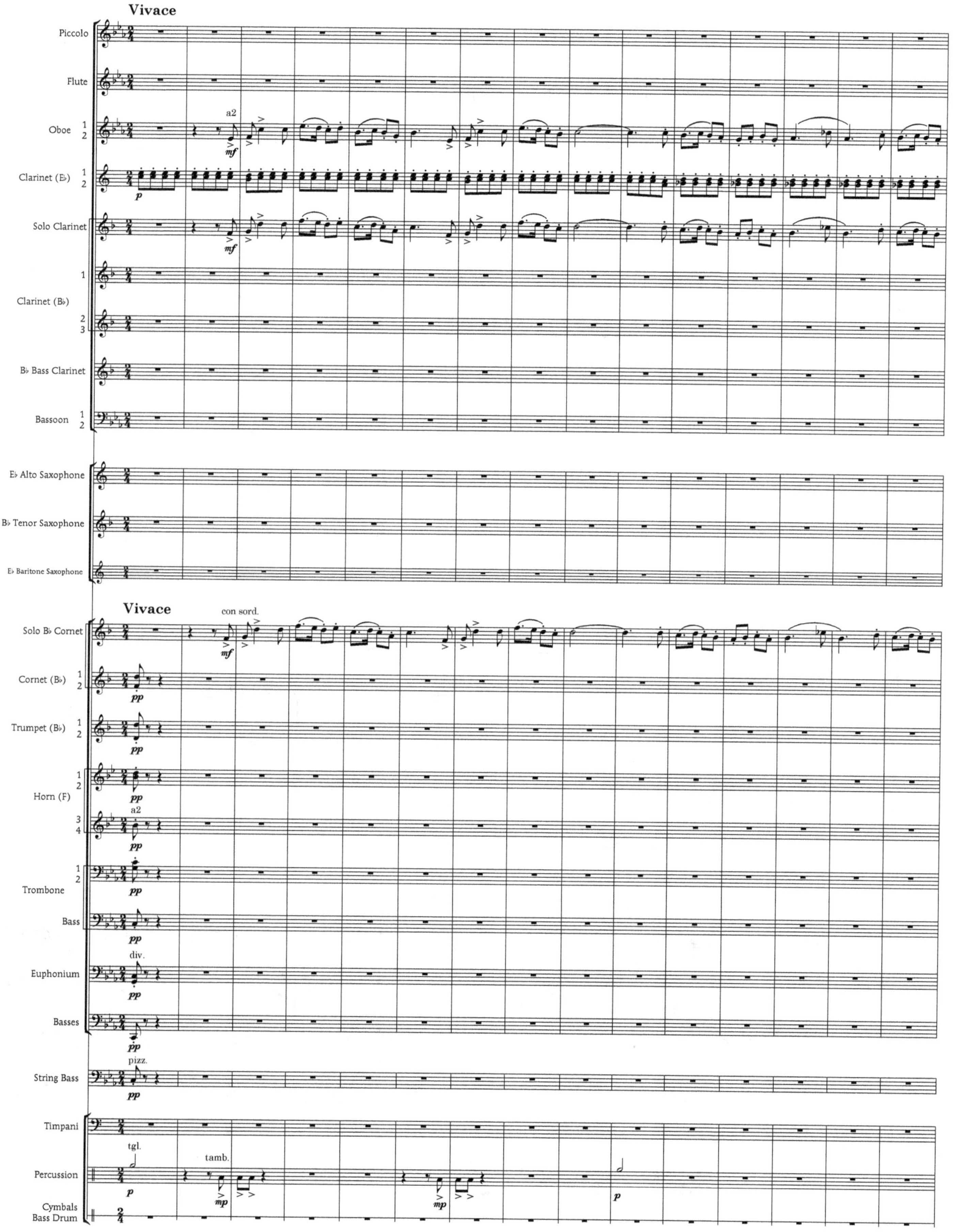

25
16
Picc.
Fl.
Ob. 1 2
E♭ Cl. 1 2
a2
Solo Cl.
Cl. 1
Cl. 2 3
a2
B. Cl.
Bn. 1 2
Alto Sax.
Ten. Sax.
Bari. Sax.
mf
p
25
16
Solo Cor.
Cor. 1 2
2. div.
1.
Tpt. 1 2
Hn. 1 2
Hn. 3 4
a2
Trb. 1 2
Bass
Eph.
div.
Basses
S. B.
arco
Timp.
Per.
Cymb. B. D.

31
Picc.
Fl.
Ob.
E♭ Cl.
Solo Cl.
Cl.
B. Cl.
Bn.
Alto Sax.
Ten. Sax.
Bari. Sax.
Solo Cor.
Cor.
Tpt.
Hn.
Trb.
Bass
Eph.
Basses
S. B.
Timp.
Per.
Cymb.
B. D.
p cresc.
cresc.
a2
ff

43
Picc.
Fl.
Ob. 1 2
E♭ Cl. 1 2
p
Solo Cl.
Cl. 1 2 3
B. Cl.
p
Bn. 1 2
p
Alto Sax.
p
Ten. Sax.
p
Bari. Sax.
43
Solo Cor.
Cor. 1 2
Tpt. 1 2
Hn. 1 2 3 4
Trb. 1 2
1.
p
Bass
Eph.
unis.
p
Basses
p
p
S. B.
pizz.
p
p
Timp.
Per.
tgl.
p
p
Cymb. B. D.

58
67 L'istesso tempo
Picc.
Fl.
Ob. 1 2
E♭ Cl. 1 2
a2
Solo Cl.
p dolce
Cl. 1 2 3
B. Cl.
Bn. 1 2
Alto Sax.
Ten. Sax.
Bari. Sax.
58
senza sord.
67 L'istesso tempo
Solo Cor.
Cor. 1 2
Tpt. 1 2
Hn. 1 2 3 4
Trb. 1 2
Bass
a2
solo
Eph.
tutti
Basses
arco
S. B.
Timp.
Per.
Cymb.
B. D.

70
Picc.
Fl.
solo
Ob. 1 2
E♭ Cl. 1 2
Solo Cl.
Cl. 1 2 3
B. Cl.
Bn. 1 2
Alto Sax.
Ten. Sax.
Bari. Sax.
Solo Cor.
Cor. 1 2
Tpt. 1 2
Hn. 1 2 3 4
Trb. 1 2 Bass
Eph.
Basses
S. B.
Timp.
Per.
Cymb. B. D.

78
83
Picc.
Fl.
Ob. 1 2
1.
E♭ Cl. 1 2
Solo Cl.
Cl. 1 2 3
p
B. Cl.
Bn. 1 2
a2
Alto Sax.
Ten. Sax.
Bari. Sax.
Solo Cor.
mf dolce
Cor. 1 2
Tpt. 1 2
Hn. 1 2 3 4
Trb. 1 2
Bass
Eph.
solo
Basses
S. B.
Timp.
Per.
Cymb. B. D.

86
Picc.
Fl.
Ob. 1 2
E♭ Cl. 1 2
Solo Cl.
Cl. 1 2 3
B. Cl.
Bn. 1 2
Alto Sax.
Ten. Sax.
Bari. Sax.
Solo Cor.
Cor. 1 2
Tpt. 1 2
Hn. 1 2 3 4
Trb. 1 2
Bass
Eph.
Basses
S. B.
Timp.
Per.
Cymb. B. D.
tutti
p
mf
pp

94
Picc.
Fl.
Ob. 1 2
a2
E♭ Cl. 1 2
1.
Solo Cl. 1
Cl. 2
3
mf
p
B. Cl.
Bn. 1 2
a2
p
Alto Sax.
Ten. Sax.
Bari. Sax.
94
Solo Cor.
Cor. 1 2
a2
mf
p
Tpt. 1 2
Hn. 1 2
3 4
Trb. 1 2
Bass
Eph.
unis.
solo
tutti
(solo)
Basses
S. B.
pizz.
Timp.
Per.
tgl.
tamb.
Cymb. B. D.

109
104
Picc.
Fl.
Ob. 1 2
a2
mf
E♭ Cl. 1 2
1.
Solo Cl.
Cl. 1 2 3
B. Cl.
Bn. 1 2
p
Alto Sax.
Ten. Sax.
Bari. Sax.
109
104
con sord.
Solo Cor.
Cor. 1 2
Tpt. 1 2
Hn. 1 2 3 4
Trb. 1 2
Bass
Eph.
Basses
arco
S. B.
Timp.
Per.
Cymb. B. D.

119
123 L'istesso tempo
Picc.
Fl.
Ob. 1 2
E♭ Cl. 1 2
a2
Solo Cl. 1
(solo)
one player
one player
Cl. 2
3
B. Cl.
Bn. 1 2
Alto Sax.
Ten. Sax.
Bari. Sax.
119
123 L'istesso tempo
Solo Cor.
Cor. 1 2
Tpt. 1 2
Hn. 1 2 3 4
Trb. 1 2
Bass
Eph.
Basses
S. B.
Timp.
Per.
Cymb. B. D.

128
Picc.
Fl.
Ob. 1 2
E♭ Cl. 1 2
Solo Cl. 1
Cl. 2
3
B. Cl.
Bn. 1 2
Alto Sax.
Ten. Sax.
Bari. Sax.
Solo Cor.
Cor. 1 2
Tpt. 1 2
Hn. 1 2
3 4
Trb. 1 2
Bass
Eph.
Basses
S. B.
Timp.
Per.
Cymb. B. D.
a2
solo
tutti
1.
div.
unis.
p
mf
pp

136
Picc.
Fl.
Ob. 1 2
E♭ Cl. 1 2
Solo Cl. 1
Cl. 2
3
B. Cl.
Bn. 1 2
Alto Sax.
Ten. Sax.
Bari. Sax.
Solo Cor.
Cor. 1 2
Tpt. 1 2
Hn. 1 2 3 4
Trb. 1 2
Bass
Eph.
Basses
S. B.
Timp.
Per.
Cymb. B. D.
morendo
a2
1.
senza sord.
solo
unis.
one player
p
pp
ppp

3. March

12
Picc.
Fl.
Ob. 1 2
E♭ Cl. 1 2
Cl. 1 2 3
B. Cl.
Bn. 1 2
Alto Sax.
Ten. Sax.
Bari. Sax.
12
Cor. 1 2
div.
unis.
Tpt. 1 2
Hn. 1 2 3 4
a2
Trb. 1 2
Bass
Eph.
Basses
S. B.
Timp.
Per.
Cymb. B. D.

24
Picc.
Fl.
Ob. 1 2
E♭ Cl. 1 2
Cl. 1 2 3
B. Cl.
Bn. 1 2
Alto Sax.
Ten. Sax.
Bari. Sax.
24
Cor. 1 2
cresc.
unis.
ff
f
Tpt. 1 2
Hn. 1 2 3 4
a2
Trb. 1 2
Bass
Eph.
Basses
S. B.
Timp.
Per.
Cymb. B. D.

36
37
Picc.
Fl.
Ob. 1 2
E♭ Cl. 1 2
a2
mf con largezza
Cl. 1 2 3
B. Cl.
Bn. 1 2
Alto Sax.
Ten. Sax.
Bari. Sax.
Cor. 1 2
ff dim.
p
Tpt. 1 2
Hn. 1 2 3 4
Trb. 1 2
Bass
dim.
Eph.
Basses
S. B.
Timp.
Per.
Cymb. B. D.
ff

49
Picc.
Fl.
Ob. 1 2
E♭ Cl. 1 2
Cl. 1 2 3
B. Cl.
Bn. 1 2
Alto Sax.
Ten. Sax.
Bari. Sax.
49
Cor. 1 2
Tpt. 1 2
Hn. 1 2 3 4
Trb. 1 2
Bass
Eph.
Basses
S. B.
Timp.
Per.
Cymb. B. D.

63
71
Picc.
Fl.
Ob. 1 2
a2
mf
E♭ Cl. 1 2
Cl. 1 2 3
B. Cl.
Bn. 1 2
Alto Sax.
Ten. Sax.
Bari. Sax.
63
71
Cor. 1 2
Tpt. 1 2
Hn. 1 2 3 4
Trb. 1 2
Bass
Eph.
Basses
S. B.
Timp.
Per.
Cymb. B. D.

77
Picc.
Fl.
Ob. 1 2
E♭ Cl. 1 2
Cl. 1 2 3
solo 1.
B. Cl.
Bn. 1 2
Alto Sax.
Ten. Sax.
Bari. Sax.
Cor. 1 2
Tpt. 1 2
Hn. 1 2 3 4
Trb. 1 2
Bass
a2
Eph.
unis.
Basses
S. B.
Timp.
Per.
tgl.
Cymb. B. D.
p

90
97
Picc.
Fl.
Ob. 1 2
E♭ Cl. 1 2
Cl. 1 2 3
B. Cl.
Bn. 1 2
Alto Sax.
Ten. Sax.
Bari. Sax.
Cor. 1 2
Tpt. 1 2
Hn. 1 2 3 4
Trb. 1 2
Bass
Eph.
Basses
S. B.
Timp.
Per.
Cymb. B. D.
dim.
a2
unis.
div.
1.
pp
p
mf

102
Picc.
Fl.
Ob. 1 2
E♭ Cl. 1 2
Cl. 1 2 3
B. Cl.
Bn. 1 2
Alto Sax.
Ten. Sax.
Bari. Sax.
Cor. 1 2
Tpt. 1 2
Hn. 1 2 3 4
Trb. 1 2
Bass
Eph.
Basses
S. B.
Timp.
Per.
Cymb. B. D.
cresc.
a2
solo
unis.
S. D.
f
mf
pp

123
114
Picc.
Fl.
Ob. 1 2
E♭ Cl. 1 2
Cl. 1 2 3
B. Cl.
Bn. 1 2
Alto Sax.
Ten. Sax.
Bari. Sax.
Cor. 1 2
Tpt. 1 2
Hn. 1 2 3 4
Trb. 1 2
Bass
Eph.
Basses
S. B.
Timp.
Per.
Cymb. B. D.
cresc.
ff
f
unis.
a2
p cresc. poco a poco

126
Picc.
Fl.
Ob. 1 2
a2
E♭ Cl. 1 2
Cl. 1 2 3
B. Cl.
Bn. 1 2
Alto Sax.
Ten. Sax.
Bari. Sax.
126
Cor. 1 2
Tpt. 1 2
Hn. 1 2 3 4
a2
a2
Trb. 1 2
Bass
Eph.
Basses
S. B.
Timp.
Per.
Cymb. B. D.

137
Picc.
Fl.
Ob. 1 2
a2
E♭ Cl. 1 2
Cl. 1 2 3
B. Cl.
Bn. 1 2
Alto Sax.
Ten. Sax.
Bari. Sax.
137
Cor. 1 2
Tpt. 1 2
Hn. 1 2 3 4
Trb. 1 2
Bass
Eph.
Basses
S. B.
Timp.
Per.
p cresc. poco a poco
ff
Cymb. B. D.

147
Picc.
Fl.
Ob. 1 2
a2
E♭ Cl. 1 2
Cl. 1 2 3
B. Cl.
Bn. 1 2
Alto Sax.
Ten. Sax.
Bari. Sax.
147
Cor. 1 2
Tpt. 1 2
Hn. 1 2 3 4
Trb. 1 2
Bass
Eph.
Basses
S. B.
Timp.
Per.
Cymb. B. D.

159
meno mosso
più mosso
Picc.
Fl.
Ob. 1 2
E♭ Cl. 1 2
Cl. 1 2 3
B. Cl.
Bn. 1 2
Alto Sax.
Ten. Sax.
Bari. Sax.
fff
159
meno mosso
più mosso
div.
unis.
a2
Cor. 1 2
Tpt. 1 2
Hn. 1 2 3 4
Trb. 1 2
Bass
Eph.
Basses
S. B.
Timp.
Per.
Cymb. B. D.
ff
ffff
with stick

42

40512